CONFERENCE PROCEEDINGS

Increasing the Capacity of Freight Transportation

U.S. and Canadian Perspectives

David S. Ortiz, Brian Weatherford, Henry H. Willis,
Myles Collins, Naveen Mandava, Chris Ordowich

Sponsored by the Paul Volcker Initiative for Public Service and the
Canadian Consulate General of Los Angeles

RAND INFRASTRUCTURE, SAFETY, AND ENVIRONMENT

The work described here was cosponsored by the Paul Volcker Initiative for Public Service at the Frederick S. Pardee RAND Graduate School and the Canadian Consulate General of Los Angeles and was conducted under the auspices of the Transportation, Space, and Technology (TST) Program within RAND Infrastructure, Safety, and Environment (ISE).

ISBN: 978-0-8330-4125-8

The RAND Corporation is a nonprofit research organization providing objective analysis and effective solutions that address the challenges facing the public and private sectors around the world. RAND's publications do not necessarily reflect the opinions of its research clients and sponsors.

Published 2007 by the RAND Corporation
1776 Main Street, P.O. Box 2138, Santa Monica, CA 90407-2138
1200 South Hayes Street, Arlington, VA 22202-5050
4570 Fifth Avenue, Suite 600, Pittsburgh, PA 15213-2665
RAND URL: http://www.rand.org/
To order RAND documents or to obtain additional information, contact
Distribution Services: Telephone: (310) 451-7002;
Fax: (310) 451-6915; Email: order@rand.org

Preface

This document synthesizes the discussions of a one-day workshop, "Increasing the Capacity of Freight Transport: Canadian and American Perspectives on the Challenges Ahead," that was held in Santa Monica, California, on February 16, 2006. The more than 30 U.S. and Canadian stakeholders in attendance, who represented modal freight carriers; manufacturers; organized labor; and local, state, provincial, and federal governments, met to discuss the declining performance of the North American freight transport system and to determine strategies for increasing freight transport capacity. Participants identified examples of the current and expected economic effects of constraints on the freight transport system; highlighted physical, contractual, and regulatory constraints on the free movement of freight; and charted a path toward addressing the most pressing issues through public-sector, private-sector, and joint action.

This document is the workshop's proceedings and should be of interest to carriers and shippers in the freight transport system and to policymakers in transportation at all levels of government. These proceedings are intended to provide guidance to those attempting to develop long-term strategies for increasing freight transport capacity while taking into account environmental and security concerns.

The workshop was cosponsored by the Paul Volcker Initiative for Public Service at the Frederick S. Pardee RAND Graduate School and the Canadian Consulate General of Los Angeles. Staff from the RAND Corporation Infrastructure, Safety, and Environment division facilitated the workshop's sessions.

The RAND Transportation, Space, and Technology Program

This research was conducted under the auspices of the Transportation, Space, and Technology (TST) Program within RAND Infrastructure, Safety, and Environment (ISE). The mission of RAND Infrastructure, Safety, and Environment is to improve the development, operation, use, and protection of society's essential physical assets and natural resources and to enhance the related social assets of safety and security of individuals in transit and in their workplaces and communities. The TST research portfolio encompasses policy areas including transportation systems, space exploration, information and telecommunication technologies, nano- and biotechnologies, and other aspects of science and technology policy.

Questions or comments about these proceedings should be sent to the project leaders, David S. Ortiz (David_Ortiz@rand.org) and Henry H. Willis (Henry_Willis@rand.org). Information about the Transportation, Space, and Technology Program is available online (http://www.rand.org/ise/tech). Inquiries about TST research should be sent to the following address:

Martin Wachs, Director
Transportation, Space, and Technology Program, ISE
RAND Corporation
1776 Main Street
P. O. Box 2138
Santa Monica, CA 90401-2138
310-393-0411, x7720
Martin_Wachs@rand.org

Contents

Tables

Summary

Disruptions are increasing in North American supply chains. The capacity of freight transportation in North America is threatening economic competitiveness. Rising shipping costs, increasingly lengthy shipping times, increasingly variable transit times, and increasingly large inventories—all of these are evidence of constraints in the freight transport system.

As North American manufacturing and retail's reliance on imports has increased, highway and rail infrastructure has been neither maintained nor expanded in critical places. Other factors, such as increased fuel prices, security requirements, border delays, and a shortage of truck drivers, are eroding the freight transport system's performance. Consequently, shippers are stocking more parts and supplies, resorting to expensive backup transportation, and revisiting facility location decisions to cope with disruptions. Although consumers have yet to feel the effects, this "brittle" (i.e., sensitive to small disruptions) freight transport system, when coupled with continuing increases in demand, may lead to continentwide economic damage.

On February 16, 2006, in Santa Monica, California, more than 30 U.S. and Canadian stakeholders representing modal freight carriers; manufacturers; organized labor; and local, state, provincial, and federal governments met to discuss the declining performance of the North American freight transport system and to determine strategies for increasing freight transport capacity. Over the course of this one-day workshop, the participants identified examples of current and expected economic effects of capacity constraints on the freight transport system. They also highlighted specific physical, contractual, and regulatory constraints to the free movement of freight and charted a path toward addressing the most pressing issues through public-sector, private-sector, and joint action. This document summarizes the workshop's discussions and the participants' consensus.

Workshop participants partitioned constraints in North American freight transportation into categories characterized by duration, frequency, and effect. Table S.1 lists the constraints according to these characteristics and provides examples.

Intermittent constraints—that is, disturbances that briefly affect freight movement and are resolved without significant intervention—are typically well understood and can be accounted for in most freight transport markets. Examples of intermittent physical constraints are local weather, accidents, and other such random events that cause delays; examples of intermittent nonphysical constraints are increased security inspections, supply chain manager errors, and short-term labor availability.

Table S.1
Constraints in the North American Freight Transport System

Type of Constraint	Duration	Frequency or Relative Probability	Effect	Physical Examples	Nonphysical Examples
Intermittent	Short	Sporadic	Local or firm	Weather Accidents Loading or unloading delays Random cargo inspections Rationing of rail and trucking capacity	Regulatory uncertainty Seasonal shipping trends Labor availability
Chronic	Medium	Often	Regional or sector	Rail capacity Port capacity Road capacity Single-mode and intermodal transfer capacity Border crossings	Labor disputes and contract renewals Security procedures Contractual limitations Managing freight transportation's impact on communities Customs and trade compliance Safety compliance
Catastrophic	Long	Rare	National or macroeconomic	Natural disaster Terrorist attack	Labor actions and strikes

Chronic constraints are emerging issues that impose additional costs on freight transport systems. Of all the chronic constraints, the critical one is the physical capacity of the intermodal transport infrastructure, though congestion at border crossings is also a significant concern. And there are a large number of nonphysical constraints—for example, labor availability, environmental regulations, and post-9/11 security procedures. The expanding list of chronic constraints in the North American freight transport system suggests that it is becoming brittle and is in need of attention.

Catastrophic constraints are those that bring the freight transport system to a halt. Fortunately, these tend to occur relatively infrequently and often only affect isolated regions. The workshop participants identified two fundamental examples of events that could cripple the system: a natural disaster, such as an earthquake or hurricane that destroys transportation assets, and a terrorist attack that destroys key infrastructure or provokes greatly increased freight transport system security procedures.

The output of the workshop was an agenda for change.[1] The first step in this agenda is to promote the most efficient use of current transport assets. Participants believe that enough additional capacity exists for the near term but that there are barriers to its most effective use. For the long term, participants recommend several steps. First, a unified view of the freight transport system must be reached so that policymakers will have a consistent framework for measuring the performance of North American freight transportation and assessing policy options. Next, to form the innovative public-private partnerships that will be needed to

[1] Proposals for bolstering and expanding the freight transport system's capacity are numerous, but, to date, none has motivated action. See Appendix D, the annotated bibliography, for brief descriptions of several recent plans for increasing North America's freight transport capacity.

address the many constraints in the system, policymakers must understand the source of the current market's apparent failure to provide adequate private investment in freight transportation. Finally, efforts must show concrete progress on some of the issues to demonstrate the importance of collective action and build support for common interests in freight transport planning.

Without action, intermittent constraints in the system are likely to become more frequent, chronic constraints more acute, and the potential damage of catastrophic constraints more devastating. Workshop participants agreed that the net result of these constraints would not be marginally increased freight costs but, instead, degradation of the competitiveness of the North American economies.

Acknowledgments

We would like to thank the people and organizations that helped make the workshop a success. The Volcker Initiative at the Pardee RAND Graduate School (PRGS) and the Canadian Consulate General, Los Angeles, provided financial sponsorship for the workshop. The staff of the consulate, Eric Pelletier and Pam Johnson, helped to engage Canadian business leaders. Ted Mackay, of the Canadian Embassy in Washington, D.C., provided critical insight on the freight policy issues facing Canada and the United States. Bianca Roberts, of PRGS, took the lead in organizing the workshop and speakers. Kristen Copeland provided key logistical support for the workshop. Rae W. Archibald, acting dean of PRGS, actively supported the workshop. RAND Vice President Michael Rich motivated the workshop participants with his excellent introduction to the issues and introduction of the workshop's speakers.

The two speakers, Captain Paul Wiedenhoeft of the U.S. Coast Guard and Ambassador Alain Dudoit, Canadian Consul General, Los Angeles, addressed critical security and trade facilitation issues facing the United States and Canada.

The workshop participants merit special thanks for their part in what was a spirited series of discussions on a critical issue facing North America. We thank, specifically, Jane Beseda, Vice President, and Tony Minyon, Director, both of Toyota Motor Sales, Inc., for providing invaluable leadership throughout the workshop's organization and execution.

We would also like to thank Jeri O'Donnell and the RAND Publications department staff for services in editing and preparing the document for publication.

Abbreviations

AMR	advance manifest rule
CALMITSAC	California Marine and Intermodal Transportation System Advisory Council
CBP	U.S. Customs and Border Protection
CSI	Container Security Initiative
C-TPAT	Customs-Trade Partnership Against Terrorism
DHS	U.S. Department of Homeland Security
DOT	U.S. Department of Transportation
FAST	Free and Secure Trade
ILWU	International Longshore and Warehouse Union
ISE	Infrastructure, Safety, and Environment
ISPS	International Ship and Port Security
LNG	liquefied natural gas
MTSA	Maritime Transportation Security Act
PRGS	Pardee RAND Graduate School
SCAG	Southern California Association of Governments
SPP	Security and Prosperity Partnership
TEU	20-foot equivalent unit
TST	Transportation, Space, and Technology
TWIC	Transportation Worker Identification Credential

CHAPTER ONE

Introduction

The U.S. economy is dependent on an efficient, robust, and adaptive freight transport system. Manufacturers rely on the freight transport system to support their supply chains, which may span multiple continents and are optimized to reduce inventory. Retailers, too, rely on an efficient and predictable freight transport system as they coordinate the flow of goods into the United States to meet seasonal consumer demand. Quite simply, modern business practice assumes that freight transportation across and within borders will be available and reliable. The assumption is starting to fail: The North American Freight transport system is running at capacity and disruptions are commonplace. Contributing to the system's sensitivity are several factors, including environmental externalities from freight transportation, community effects, labor shortages and disputes, and security concerns. In February 2006, RAND convened a select group of public and private decisionmakers in freight transportation to discuss the economic effects of the North American freight transport system's declining performance and options for increasing the system's capacity.

Modern manufacturing is dependent entirely on the structure and operation of firms' supply chains. Throughout the 1980s and 1990s, U.S. manufacturers focused on their core areas of expertise, outsourcing components and subsystems to suppliers (National Research Council, 2000; Womack and Jones, 1996). The amount of work that is subcontracted to suppliers is one way to measure firms' dependence on their supply chains: In the defense industry, the total product cost that was subcontracted grew from an average of 9 percent in the 1950s to 43 percent in the 1990s (National Research Council, 2000). In the development of its new passenger airliner, the 787, Boeing is subcontracting the production of complete subsystems to suppliers throughout the world; it claims that 65 percent of the production is performed by subcontractors (Mecham, 2006). Cross-border manufacturing is common in the auto industry, and the Ambassador Bridge, which connects Windsor, Ontario, to Detroit, Michigan, is a key link in what has been called the "NAFTA Corridor" (Ryan, 2005). Factories near the southern U.S. border known as maquiladoras produce goods exclusively for the U.S. market, capitalizing on proximity to the United States and lower labor costs in Mexico. Transpacific trade can be thought of as a "supply chain corridor" in addition to one delivering finished products (White, 2006). Dell Inc. carries no inventory and dynamically balances production with orders such that customers receive its products as quickly as possible (Breen, 2004), a practice known as just-in-time production.

Underlying this modern business practice is an assumption that freight transportation will be available. For manufacturers to support the just-in-time model, the flow of raw materials and work-in-progress inventory across the border and throughout the country must be predictable in time and cost. For retailers, the requirement for freight transportation varies seasonally, with more needed during the summer and early fall during preparation for the holiday shopping season and less needed during the winter and spring. Competing for freight transportation are commodities: Coal and grain travel by rail and barge (Frittelli 2005); perishable agricultural products typically travel by refrigerated truck or train and must compete for capacity.

The conditions under which the freight transport system in North America can support an expanding economy based on the just-in-time model are degrading. U.S. transportation infrastructure is breaking down: The American Society of Civil Engineers gave rail, roads, bridges, waterways, and aviation "grades" of C or below (American Society of Civil Engineers, 2005). The freight transport system is operating at full capacity for much of the year. Operating at capacity makes maintenance and expansion of the system difficult and leads to chronic delays in the shipment and receipt of goods. Freight rail capacity in the United States and Canada is limited and rail system performance is deteriorating. For example, intermodal freight competes with commodities such as grain and coal for locomotives and transit, but commodities are typically not as time-sensitive as intermodal freight (Pinkston, 2006). Performance of intermodal shipping via freight rail has declined in terms of average cross-continental transit time and shipments typically arrive several days late (Widdows, 2005). Performance has continued to decline despite significant investments in track, locomotives, and facilities by U.S. Class I railroads (Koraleski, 2005); railroads claim that the cost of capital to maintain and improve infrastructure exceeds return on investment by over 5 percent (Koraleski, 2005). Despite poor performance, fuel surcharges and increased freight demand have allowed U.S. Class I railroads to continue to raise prices (Seidl and Ghuman, 2006).

Congestion throughout the North American freight transport system is common. Trucking firms do fund indirectly the construction and maintenance of the U.S. interstate highway system, but they must contend with the congestion, which is leading increasingly to delays (Njord and Meyer, 2006). In autumn 2004, congestion at the ports of Los Angeles and Long Beach led to the diversion of more than 100 container vessels to other ports; the backups also snarled local traffic (Mongelluzzo, 2004). Secretary of Transportation Norman Y. Mineta, has noted that congestion "threatens supply chain efficiencies" and recently called for a national effort to reduce congestion, which would include identifying key transportation corridors, convening diverse stakeholders, working with border officials to speed crossings, and engaging shippers and carriers directly (U.S. Department of Transportation, 2006a). Furthermore, U.S. port capacity may not be able to accommodate the projected growth in trade with Asia (Knatz, 2005).

Ocean carriers, however, do not face a capacity crunch. In a continued effort to reduce unit costs, carriers have ordered containerships capable of carrying 10,000 20-foot equivalent units (TEUs) (the standard unit of trade in containerized shipping) (Foschi, 2004). As these vessels enter service, ocean carriers find that there is overcapacity in their fleets, which has led to a decline in freight shipping rates for ocean transport; at the same time, ports and highways remain congested and trade growth is expected to continue (White, 2006). Ever-larger containerships lead to increased port traffic, which, in turn, leads to investments in infrastructure and facilities by other modes of transportation. Railroads have responded to the growth of trade by focusing on critical corridors, double-tracking routes from Los Angeles to Chicago (Machalaba, 2004), while abandoning other parts of their networks: U.S. railways service fewer markets with intermodal ramps and operate fewer track miles than in 1960 or 1990 (Lofgren, 2005).

Port and shipping security remains a critical concern. In response to the attacks of September 11, 2001, a number of regulations and programs have been instituted in the United States and worldwide. These security programs and measures include the International Maritime Organization's promulgation of the International Ship and Port Security (ISPS) code in 2002 and the U.S. counterpart to the ISPS, the Maritime Transportation Security Act (MTSA) of 2002. Both codes institute a wide set of measures to improve vessel and port security, and both went into effect on July 1, 2004.[1] The Container Security Initiative (CSI) is a program that stations U.S. Customs and Border Protection (CBP) agents at foreign ports to inspect cargo before it is loaded onto a U.S.-bound vessel.[2] Under the 24-hour advance manifest rule (AMR), carriers must submit a manifest for all U.S.-bound cargo 24 hours before the cargo is loaded onto a vessel.[3] Similarly, vessels seeking to call at a U.S. port must notify the U.S. Coast Guard of their arrival 96 hours beforehand.[4] The Customs-Trade Partnership Against Terrorism (C-TPAT) is a voluntary program in which shippers and carriers certify that they and their suppliers adhere to certain security procedures and standards. In return for their participation, the shipments of C-TPAT participants are regarded as lower risk than other shipments and therefore are less likely to be inspected, speeding their flow through the port of entry. C-TPAT participants include all major U.S. importers and international carriers.[5] In designing these and other security measures and programs, CBP has taken into account concerns by the trade community that heavy-handed security could slow trade and have a significant adverse economic effect.

However, security programs and responses compound capacity constraints. For example, the capacity of the Ambassador Bridge, which links Windsor, Ontario, with Detroit, Michigan, is so limited that there are reports of the operator "waving through" hundreds of vehicles without any security check simply to clear backlogs (Audi, 2006). In a recent debate over new port security legislation, some lawmakers proposed that all containers entering the country be nonintrusively inspected using scanning equipment, a proposal that was regarded as infeasible given technological and physical constraints at ports ("The Right Kind of Security," 2006; Martonosi, Ortiz, and Willis, 2005).

---

[1] For more information on the ISPS code, see International Maritime Organization (undated). For more information on the MTSA, see U.S. Coast Guard (undated).

[2] For more information on the CSI, see U.S. Customs and Border Protection (undated[b]).

[3] For more information on the 24-hour AMR, see Byrd (2004).

[4] For more information on the 24-hour advance notice of arrival, see U.S. Department of Homeland Security (2004).

[5] For more information on C-TPAT, see U.S. Customs and Border Protection (undated[a]).

The effects of freight transportation have become a significant issue. For example, the ports of Los Angeles and Long Beach in San Pedro Bay are the largest source of airborne emissions in the area. A report by the California Air Resources Board estimated that emissions from the ports were a significant contributor to health problems in the area surrounding the port complex (Tran, 2006). The local community has demanded action and has become involved in the planning process at the ports, and the ports have responded (Schoch, 2006): Programs include alternative fuels for vessels entering the area, the availability of shore power to obviate the need to idle marine engines, and extended gate hours to reduce congestion and idling vehicles (PierPASS, undated; Port of Long Beach, 2005). Environmental concerns are addressed explicitly in California's plan to improve freight transportation (California Environmental Protection Agency Air Resources Board, 2005; California Environmental Protection Agency, 2005). The effects of freight transportation on communities are an international issue. In Windsor, Ontario, the local highway ends several kilometers before the Ambassador Bridge, forcing traffic onto city streets (Ryan, 2005); community groups are involved closely with efforts to expand capacity in this area (Schwartz, 2005).

Labor is an ongoing issue in freight transportation. From September 27 to October 9, 2002, port owners and operators locked the gates of their facilities along the western coast of the United States, shutting them down for business. The contract with the International Longshore and Warehouse Union (ILWU) had expired on July 1, 2002, and the lockout and resulting shutdown were widely expected. Shippers and carriers made contingency plans, to the extent possible, to cope with the loss of the majority of the U.S. import capacity. Some cargo was rerouted, through the Panama Canal and around South America, to ports on the East Coast. Other shippers anticipated the event, advancing orders by several weeks or delaying them until the parties had resolved the dispute (Hall, 2004).[6] As global trade continues to increase, shortages of stevedores are expected (Finnegan, 2006). The trucking industry faces a shortage of drivers, possibly because of the lifestyle and also because of the pay, which has not advanced in real terms recently (Lofgren, 2005). Since transportation workers have access to critical infrastructure, labor is also considered a security issue. Background checks for drivers of hazardous materials are now required, and recent legislation now requires the U.S. Department of Homeland Security (DHS) to implement the Transportation Worker Identification Credential (TWIC) program for all port workers (U.S. House of Representatives, undated).

The North American freight transport system is already a public-private enterprise. The U.S. interstate highway system is now 50 years old and was constructed with federal and state resources. As the system ages and states look to alternative sources of funds for system maintenance and expansion, portions of the system are being leased to private companies (Goldstein, 2006). Since deregulation in the 1970s, the private sector owns, operates, and maintains U.S. freight railroads. Municipalities typically own U.S. ports, but private companies most often perform operations at major container ports (Finnegan, 2006). Airfreight facilities are privately owned and maintained, but they are located strategically to take advantage of local (public) highways and (private) rail corridors; United Parcel Service, for example, uses truck and rail

[6] Dell, for instance, anticipated the event and chartered 18 Boeing 747s from various carriers to ship parts from Asia to the United States, enabling it to continue operations while absorbing the additional transport cost (Breen, 2004).

transport extensively, has built a private network of regional facilities, and is expanding its facility in Louisville, Kentucky (City of Louisville, 2006). Manufacturers and retailers locate their facilities to have easy access to freight transport infrastructure and markets, as manifested by the prevalence of distribution centers in Southern California.

Public policy with respect to freight transportation has lagged behind the integrated structure and operations of the freight transport system. In general, policy is based on single modes, with a bureaucracy organized similarly. Earlier this year, the U.S. Department of Transportation (DOT) released a framework for a national freight policy (2006a) that outlines objectives for improving the performance of the U.S. freight transportation system in general, but actual policy solutions do not yet exist.

As a first step in quantifying the effects of these trends in the freight transport system and in formulating long-term policy solutions to improve the system's performance, RAND Infrastructure, Safety, and Environment (ISE), a division of the RAND Corporation, convened a one-day workshop of private-sector and public-sector leaders. The Canadian Consulate General and the Volcker Initiative for Public Service of the Pardee RAND Graduate School (PRGS) cosponsored this event, which took place on February 16, 2006, in Santa Monica, California. This document is the workshop's proceedings; it summarizes the discussions and the conclusions.

Following this first introductory chapter are two chapters summarizing the discussions in which the trends are addressed as capacity constraints on North American freight transportation: Chapter Two summarizes workshop discussions regarding economic effects of constraints on the freight transport system; Chapter Three describes critical constraints as workshop participants viewed them. The document concludes with a summary of participants' views on the next steps for policy and supporting analysis to improve the performance of the North American freight transport system. Four appendixes present the workshop agenda, the comments of Ambassador Alain Dudoit, the list of attendees, and an annotated bibliography of recent relevant studies and plans, respectively.

CHAPTER TWO

Economic Consequences of Capacity Constraints in North American Freight Transportation: The Move to Just-In-Case Logistics

Chapters Two through Four summarize discussions from the one-day workshop cosponsored by PRGS and the Canadian Consulate General. Unless otherwise indicated, all comments are to be attributed to the workshop participants.

Bilateral commerce, supported by integrated transport networks, is a key component of the relationship between the United States and Canada. North American freight transportation supports the world's largest economic trading region. Bilateral trade between the United States and Canada is worth $590 billion per year. The United States exports more to Canada than to the European Union, and Canada's trade with the United States exceeds its trade with all other nations combined.

Capacity constraints on the North American freight transport system are having a detrimental effect on the U.S., Canadian, and Mexican economies. Specific symptoms—the questionable availability of freight transportation, the increase in time to ship goods, and the increase in shipment-time variability—indicate that these constraints are present within the system. The effects of these constraints on shippers vary: For example, rates are increasing despite the availability of transportation, and businesses, unable to plan for the variability in shipments, have to increase their inventories. In addition, limited capacity in the freight transport system is having a long-term effect on investment: Because factories and distribution centers must have access to reliable transportation, firms are viewing constraints within the transport system as a reason to delay plans for new facilities.

To understand the effects of capacity constraints in North American freight transportation, it is helpful to know about the freight transport system's recent evolution. Over the past several decades, the system's speed and reliability regularly increased and improved, allowing manufacturers and retailers to reduce their inventories, thereby liberating capital for other investments. Today, just-in-time manufacturing and lean inventory management are necessary conditions for operating a competitive firm, and firms are constantly seeking new ways to reduce their inventories. Freight carriers have responded by offering a range of services linked to this operating environment. They have also offered lower and lower rates, facilitated by declining fuel prices and their own efforts to optimize resource utilization.

Manufacturers and retailers are now discovering that inexpensive and reliable transportation is no longer available. In terms of cost and reliability, freight transportation performance is declining. And many factors are driving this decline, such as increasing fuel prices, a shortage of truck drivers, deferred maintenance on U.S. highways and freight rail systems, and limited system capacity. Just-in-time operation and lean inventories rely on a responsive and reliable supply chain.

Constraints on the freight transport system lead to delays and uncertainty and directly affect all stakeholders' costs and performance. For example, a major auto manufacturer regularly exercises contingency plans for shifting the shipment of certain components to airfreight when there is a disruption in the containerized shipping system. This manufacturer does not pass along the additional cost to its customers. Further, delays at major crossings of the Canadian and Mexican borders are frequent, periodically causing the partial shutdown of operations at factories near the border. Costly overtime operations are often required to make up the lost production. Again, consumers have yet to pay the costs of many of these disruptions.

As capacity constraints in the freight transport system grow, system disruptions become more frequent and severe. Growing uncertainty about supply chain reliability is causing some managers to reconsider just-in-time processes; in fact, workshop participants felt that current operational plans were more appropriately termed *just-in-case* logistics. Just-in-case operations require that larger inventories be maintained to compensate for the increased variance in transport times and decreased reliability in the supply chain. Workshop participants described the potential movement to a just-in-case inventory management system as a significant economic threat to the competitiveness of North American manufacturing and to the economy in general.

The 2002 West Coast port lockout, which resulted from a labor dispute, significantly affected the U.S. and Canadian economies and had long-term implications for shippers and carriers. The lockout taught carriers and shippers that the freight transport system had little capacity for handling the displaced shipments. Congestion occurred at alternative ports and on westbound road and rail connections. Vessels that could not be diverted were forced to anchor off the U.S. West Coast and wait for the dispute to be resolved. Workshop participants noted that several months passed before the system returned to normal operation. In other words, an 11-day labor dispute resulted in a several-month disruption of freight transport networks.

The lockout's effects illustrate some of the freight transport system's weaknesses. Participants described the system as "brittle," meaning its operation is sensitive to small disruptions. There is little excess capacity for most of the year, and there is none during the peak season. Additionally, peak season, which had typically occurred from late August through mid-November in anticipation of the winter shopping season, now begins at the end of June. A minor disruption in the system can cause a serious crisis. Since this type of crisis is now expected, the private sector is devoting resources to managing the events: Whenever the supply chain gets disrupted, teams of people are required to reroute cargo and alter production and shipping schedules. Since such "crises" in the freight transport system are now considered business as usual, too many resources are being devoted to reacting to them.

Workshop participants suspected that constraints in the supply chain would become more pronounced, leading to a continentwide loss of economic efficiency. The quest to reduce unit costs among intermodal carriers will have long-term effects on the system's operation. Ocean carriers are taking delivery of container ships with capacities of 10,000 TEUs, which have a draft too deep for all but a few ports, specifically Los Angeles and Long Beach, California; Seattle and Tacoma, Washington; and Norfolk, Virginia (Foschi, 2004); previous-generation vessels had capacities of approximately 6,000 TEUs and were able to call at most U.S. ports. Rail carriers are responding too, focusing their investments on expanding the capacity of major routes and deferring maintenance on less-used parts of their networks. Additional security measures and continued labor-availability problems may contribute to the problem. Workshop participants feared that North American competitiveness would suffer as disturbances increase freight transport costs in general.

The general conclusion of the workshop participants was that the tightening of the freight transport system's capacity ultimately puts North American prosperity at risk. Significant investments in freight transport infrastructure are required of the public and private sectors. Given the current and expected costs of the existing, fragmented policy, a proactive suite of investments and policies is required to address the constraints in the freight transport system. As these capacity constraints are relieved, the flow of trade in North America will improve, and that in itself should generate positive economic benefits.

CHAPTER THREE

Critical Constraints in the North American Freight Transport System

As imports from Asia and trade throughout North America increase, both the public and private sectors will need to pay attention to capacity constraints in the freight transport system. Identifying where these constraints exist in the system and developing a comprehensive understanding of how they affect shippers, carriers, and operators is an important precursor to any discussion about how to relieve the resulting congestion and uncertainty about improvements (e.g., who will make them, how they will be financed). The freight transport system is tightly interconnected, which means that congestion in one location may be caused by constraints in another.

Table 3.1 organizes constraints in the freight transport system according to duration, relative frequency, and effect.[1]

Table 3.1
Constraints in the North American Freight Transport System

Type of Constraint	Duration	Frequency or Relative Probability	Effect	Physical Examples	Nonphysical Examples
Intermittent	Short	Sporadic	Local or firm	Weather Accidents Loading or unloading delays Random cargo inspections Rationing of rail and trucking capacity	Regulatory uncertainty Seasonal shipping trends Labor availability
Chronic	Medium	Often	Regional or sector	Rail capacity Port capacity Road capacity Single-mode and intermodal transfer capacity Border crossings	Labor disputes and contract renewals Security procedures Contractual limitations Managing freight transportation's impact on communities Customs and trade compliance Safety compliance
Catastrophic	Long	Rare	National or macroeconomic	Natural disaster Terrorist attack	Labor actions and strikes

[1] The taxonomy of constraints has been expanded from one proposed by a workshop participant.

Intermittent Constraints

Intermittent constraints are short-term events that delay or disrupt the movement of freight during transport. These events are frequent enough to be predictable and often part of normal operations. An alternative view of intermittent constraints is that they exist regardless of a transport system's robustness.

Intermittent physical constraints tend to be events beyond the shipper's or carrier's control. Adverse weather and accidents are the most frequent intermittent physical constraints. Others are, for example, loading and unloading delays that occur when a particular shipment is not available at the expected time for an arbitrary reason (including yard delays), delays of the small proportion of inbound containers that are selected randomly for scanning or hand inspection, and delays resulting because carriers ration their capacity among customers.

Nonphysical intermittent constraints are those that reduce the flow of freight even though the transport system's physical capacity and ability would typically provide a higher flow of goods. For example, freight carriers and shippers sometimes alter operations temporarily pending anticipated decisions by the government, and the seasonal increase of the flow of goods can temporarily overwhelm the system's capacity. Labor availability exacerbates problems.

Although not listed in the temporary category in Table 3.1, natural disasters can also impose intermittent constraints on the freight transport system. Preparations for the arrival of Hurricane Rita included shutting down several petroleum refineries in the area surrounding Houston, Texas. After the hurricane, operators were able to restore the refining capacity quickly. Temporary disruptions due to natural disasters such as this are typically local or regional in nature (catastrophic natural disasters are discussed below).

Chronic Constraints

Compared with the temporary constraints, chronic constraints are far more problematic, and the prevalence of so many of them in the North American freight transport system indicates that the system's performance is declining.

Workshop participants uniformly agreed that intermodal rail capacity, links, and operations are significant chronic constraints in the system. Even though the U.S. freight rail network is commonly thought of as an integrated system, it is really several different networks subdivided among the mainline carriers, each operating independently. Typically, one or two mainline carriers service a given port, which reduces the options for ocean carriers and shippers. As demand for intermodal rail transportation has increased, shippers claim that railroads have raised rates but have not increased quality of service.

Mainline railroads are investing in new infrastructure, but these investments have not yet relieved congestion and improved service. Participants in the workshop believed that the margin on freight rail is not sufficient to finance the investments in new infrastructure that are required. One factor in the railroads' decisionmaking is uncertainty about future regulations, taxes, and fees. In general, the problem appears to be that the expected return on investment for new rail capacity is not high enough to compensate the railroads for the risk and uncertainty involved.

Several other concerns about rail capacity were also discussed. There is little cooperation among mainline railroads to manage the rail network as an integrated system. Individual railroads manage their own networks to maximize their revenue; in so doing, they may ration capacity or allocate traffic for some kinds of freight over others, thereby degrading the whole system's performance, participants claimed. Canada has regulations that require the railroads to make capacity available for certain kinds of freight, such as grain. Like all businesses, railroads seek to maximize use of their infrastructure, which can require their customers to make operational changes. For example, railroads are now limiting the time during which intermodal shipments may await pickup.

Although workshop participants did not perceive port capacity as a significant problem, they did view intermodal access to ports this way. The productivity at U.S. ports (measured in terms of containers handled per acre of space) is much lower than the productivity at leading ports throughout the world. Increasing U.S. port productivity would require the cooperation of organized labor, something workshop participants viewed as a tractable challenge. Participants claimed that the chronic problems with import capacity have to do with intermodal transfer capacity. Seasonal congestion is becoming progressively worse, too.

The trend toward larger container ships is expected to create significant constraints at several North American ports. Due to their deep draft, the largest container ships may call only at Los Angeles and Long Beach, Seattle and Tacoma, and Norfolk, Virginia. These vessels will require much more time to offload and load while in port and will further stress intermodal infrastructure in the port areas.

Most freight in North America travels by truck, and trucking capacity, too, is limited. Outside of urban areas, North American highway infrastructure is quite sufficient, though weather and accidents contribute to the variability of shipments traveling via truck. The principal physical constraints are border crossings and urban highways. The Ambassador Bridge, which connects Windsor, Ontario, and Detroit, Michigan, is viewed as the most significant constraint in the system. The 710 freeway in Los Angeles, which is a critical link from the Los Angeles/Long Beach port complex to the interstate highway system, is also a constraint on the flow of goods. Both of these connectors are already operating beyond their intended capacities and are inadequate for supporting the traffic associated with increased trade.

Nonphysical constraints exacerbate the physical constraints already in the system. These include labor availability, environmental regulations, local externalities and community concerns of freight transportation (noise and pollution, for example), security and trade compliance, safety, and contractual limitations.

Maintaining a workforce within the freight transport sector is becoming increasingly difficult. Working with the key unions, including the ILWU on the West Coast and the International Longshoremen's Union on the East Coast, will be essential. Labor is a key component of any effort to increase port productivity. Security concerns also play an important role in that workers' background checks and security training are expensive.

Truckers are also in short supply. Again, new security regulations and procedures exacerbate the problem because there are financial costs and delays for proper training and background checks. The trucking industry is becoming creative in responding to its labor shortages. Some carriers reported that they are migrating from the standard owner-operator model to one in which they take a more active role in recruiting, training, and certifying drivers and in financing their tractors. These tactics help to maintain a base of supply, but they do not necessarily address seasonal labor shortages.

Market uncertainties also generate capacity constraints in the freight transport system. Carriers stated that general uncertainty about the long time horizon required to pay back the capital investments necessary made them hesitant to upgrade their infrastructures. Industry is taking a wait-and-see stance on investments in new infrastructure because of the uncertainty related to security procedures and requirements.

Government regulations and processes often vary among federal, state, regional, and local agencies; the result is additional costs to communicate with and meet the requirements of the different jurisdictions, as well as incompatible regulations (such as weight and height limitations and requirements for hazardous materials for trucks). Participants reported that the process of relieving physical constraints is subject to complicated and fragmented government regulation. For example, to widen a highway, construct a new intermodal facility, or add parallel track requires that dozens of agencies and multiple jurisdictions be coordinated.

The need to protect the natural and human environment while increasing the capacity of freight transportation highlights the challenge of dealing with many agencies and organizations. Local communities and environmental advocacy groups should have a voice in any proposed expansion of freight transportation. Noise and emissions often increase with congestion, and the workshop participants felt that the best way to relieve these environmental externalities of transportation is to add capacity and expand hours of service. There is also the challenge of working with port communities to reduce environmental effects and health-related risks to the community from a number of sources. Examples are the widening of the Windsor-Detroit border crossing, the recent effort to build a liquefied natural gas (LNG) facility in Southern California, and the request by one port community that cranes not block the view of the water. Workshop participants faulted themselves for not communicating more directly with the affected communities on the economic benefits of freight transportation.

Many freight operators and carriers sign contracts that guarantee a certain level of capacity and access to the transport system. These contracts reduce risk to shippers under normal conditions. However, given the prevalence of disruptions, contracts can lead to inefficient allocation of resources by restricting flexibility in crisis situations.

Participants reported that new security procedures and requirements are exacerbating the constraints within the current freight transport system. C-TPAT was viewed as a good approach, but concerns regarding the program include limited U.S. jurisdiction and the difficulty in quantifying benefits resulting from participation. CSI is helping to reduce bottlenecks caused by security procedures at U.S. ports, but the lack of resources at foreign ports limits its effectiveness. The Automated Commercial Environment, a system to facilitate trade compliance and enhance security, is proceeding slowly. Additional uncertainty and disruption are created whenever the terror alert level rises, because these increases are accompanied by greater congestion at border crossings. And considerable uncertainty about the deployment of TWIC,[2] which is intended to authenticate all transport workers, remains. Workshop participants did not call for fewer security procedures; rather, they hoped for more cooperation between the public and private sectors.

Catastrophic Constraints

Workshop participants believed that the North American freight transport system is operating at or close to capacity, and, as is true for the electricity grid, certain disruptions can cause the system to stop working. Natural disasters most often create severe disruptions in the freight transport network that can last for months or years; sometimes, however, their effects can be catastrophic. Hurricane Katrina damaged the port of New Orleans, the Louisiana Off-Shore Oil Port, rail links, highways, and pipelines in the region. Hurricane Rita had the potential to destroy much of the U.S. refining capacity. The 1994 Northridge earthquake derailed trains and collapsed several highway bridges. These events have caused costly disruptions to the freight transport system, but, to date, none has caused the system to collapse. However, an earthquake of sufficient magnitude in Southern California could cause immense damage to the North American economy by cutting off the major U.S. connection to trade with Asia.

A terrorist attack on the freight transport system could create similar widespread damage to the economy. Although an attack on a critical node may not in and of itself cause significant damage, the response to such an attack may be to close U.S. ports and borders, which could have widespread effects. Plans for managing such security incidents and "restarting" the freight transport system do not yet exist.

A Systems Approach to Freight Transport Policy

To relieve the constraints in the freight transport system, participants argued that policymakers must employ a systems approach to quantify constraints and their effects. The North American freight transport system is tightly interconnected and currently operating at or close to capacity. The result is that constraints in one location or mode propagate quickly through the system, adversely affecting all stakeholders. Single-point solutions are unlikely to improve the system's performance. To be appropriate, policy aimed at bolstering the freight transport system needs to take into account the interrelationships among the modes and the related issues that affect the system's performance.

Participants felt that dealing with the system's primary constraints will require investments in the innovative use of existing physical infrastructure, expansion in selected regions, and additional modal interconnections. Improving physical infrastructure and managing the impact of freight transportation on communities were the most pressing chronic constraints.

Freight transportation's effects on communities have become increasingly important considerations. Any evaluation must include the effects of changes on noise, environment, and

---

[2] More information on the TWIC program is available from Transportation Security Administration (undated).

quality of life in communities through which freight passes. As increased pressure mounts to expand ports, rail systems, and highway systems, adequately addressing community concerns will become more important.

Workshop participants viewed concerns about labor shortages as secondary to constraints of physical infrastructure and management of freight transportation's impact on communities. The consensus was that the way to overcome labor shortages is to address questions of compensation and lifestyle for transportation workers. Solutions to labor shortages thus do not necessarily require changes that would produce outcomes counter to the goals of increasing freight transportation, something that is less true for physical infrastructure and community impact. That is why labor shortages are viewed as a serious but not intractable problem that markets can eventually address.

Finally, even though security is the issue driving most freight transport policy today, it is, on a day-to-day basis, the issue of least concern to workshop participants. Shippers and carriers have integrated new security procedures into processes and either absorbed costs or passed them on to customers. The effects that security may have on the decreasing reliability of shipments are seen as contributing factors to, rather than root causes of, the physical infrastructure constraints. Their greatest security concern is the potential for a large security failure to lead to extended disruptions in freight transportation. In such an event, security is expected to become an even stronger motivator of policy and a greater concern among shippers and carriers.

CHAPTER FOUR

Creating Strategies for Expanding Freight Transport Capacity in North America

Workshop participants agree that the capacity of the North American freight transport system needs to be expanded to meet current peak demand and to absorb future demand as international trade continues to increase. Shippers are experiencing increasing delays and decreasing reliability in the freight transport system. As a result of these experiences, shippers are building up larger inventories than they did in the recent past, which tends to negate efficiency gains realized through the just-in-time operations and lean inventories of previous decades. Carriers have outgrown their current infrastructure, and critical connections among modes do not have the capacity to meet the growth in demand being brought about by imports. Numerous regulatory and economic factors limit the construction of new infrastructure. In intercontinental land transportation, relatively few border crossings account for the majority of trade among North American countries. The result is a system that is not only operating at capacity but is also "brittle"—that is, sensitive to small disturbances. The economic effects will worsen if broad action is not taken to expand the system's capacity.

With the exception of events of international magnitude—the West Coast port lockout of 2002 and the West Coast congestion of 2004—the gradually declining performance of the entire freight transport system continues to go unnoticed by consumers. But increased delays and congestion are receiving attention among workshop participants and their peers, opening a window for policy action. The workshop participants agreed that long-term solutions will be put into action only if carriers and shippers use this window of opportunity to communicate their concerns about rising costs and uncertainty to policymakers and the public. Discussions during the workshop identified several possible policy windows, clarified how real costs can be anticipated, and provided early direction toward a shared voice.

Opportunities for Policy Action and Current Proposals

Increased prices or the unavailability of certain imported goods and commodities will open wider a policy window for proactive action to increase freight transport capacity. Workshop participants generally agreed that security is the issue that has most captured the attention of federal and state decisionmakers setting regulatory and funding priorities. Thus, security affords an opportunity, but not one that necessarily focuses on solutions addressing the broader issues of freight transportation.

There are many proposals for increasing freight transport capacity, but so far none has led to policy action.[1] For example, DOT released a framework for a national freight policy (U.S. Department of Transportation, 2006a) that restates the challenges and proposes common goals for the freight transport system. The national freight policy is broader than DOT's historic role of building and financing transport infrastructure. An interagency effort is needed if the full range of environmental, economic, security, and labor issues that are at stake are to be considered.

The United States, Canada, and Mexico participate in the Security and Prosperity Partnership of North America,[2] which includes more than 300 individual proposals to enhance trade and security throughout the continent. The partnership's intent and scope match the dimensions of the freight capacity constraints. However, the partnership has not moved from being a diplomatic agreement to being a tool for action and change. Perhaps because of the partnership's large number of initiatives, workshop participants were concerned that the partnership, in its current state, is too diffuse to be a basis for a focused policy to increase freight transport capacity.

A Consensus for Change

The workshop participants concluded that the first step necessary to relieve the constraints is to define the problem clearly. The North American freight transport system is ubiquitous and involves thousands of public-sector and private-sector participants, each of which views the system through the lens of its own particular expertise. Consequently, there is no consistent view on what the freight transport system is, how to measure its performance, and how to rank alternative policy options.

Build a Common View

A unified view of the freight transport system must first be developed. Such a framework would quantify the relationships and dependencies among public-sector and private-sector stakeholders, define the performance measures that are the ultimate goals of policy, and demarcate the decision space for freight transport policy. Policymakers would then be able to use this framework to quantify the effects of the current inaction, determine how congestion and security are related, and evaluate alternative long-term solutions.

Use Current Resources Effectively

Some components of effective policy do not require additional analysis. All workshop participants agreed that there was enough capacity in the freight transport system to accommodate economic growth in the near term. In many cases, regulatory and other constraints limit the

[1] See Appendix D, the annotated bibliography, for brief descriptions of several recent plans for increasing the freight transport capacity in North America.

[2] More information on this partnership is available from Security and Prosperity Partnership of North America (undated).

complete use of resources. It was agreed that policy actions seeking to increase the use of current assets should be pursued vigorously; expanded hours of operation at port facilities is one example.

Work Together

There appears to be a market failure with respect to financing the expansion of freight transport capacity. Given that the system has problems and there are clear benefits to expanding it, why is there so little investment? Because the private sector is unlikely to devote resources to areas where economic gain is uncertain, it is critical that the risks and rewards related to investments in freight transport infrastructure be characterized, especially as policymakers seek creative public-private partnerships.

Action Is Required

The previous chapter described constraints to the freight transport system as temporary (disturbances caused by exogenous events such as the weather), chronic (known problems that are tolerated despite the consequences), and catastrophic (disturbances that can bring the system to a halt). If action is not taken to address the system's problems, intermittent disturbances are likely to become chronic, and chronic problems might become catastrophic, seriously affecting the North American economy and reducing its competitive advantage.

APPENDIX A

Agenda of Workshop on Increasing the Capacity of Freight Transportation

8:30 Welcoming Remarks
Michael Rich, Executive Vice President, RAND Corporation

8:45 Keynote: A Coast Guard Perspective on Security of Freight and the Maritime Transportation System
Captain Paul Wiedenhoeft, Deputy Commander, Alternate Captain of the Port, and Alternate Federal Maritime Security Coordinator for the U.S. Coast Guard's Sector Los Angeles–Long Beach

9:45 Break

10:00 Breakout Session 1: Economic Consequences of Capacity Constraints
How do constraints in the freight transport infrastructure manifest themselves? The first session will seek to discover the effects of capacity constraints. Critical issues include reduced reliability and increased variability of shipments, requirements to increase inventory and carryings costs, effects on operating schedules and labor requirements, and ways in which capacity constraints may be measured and tracked.

11:20 Breakout Session 2: Critical Constraints in Freight Transport Networks
Where are the bottlenecks? The second session will seek to discover where in the United States and Canadian freight transport systems' capacity constraints exist. Participants will apply the results of the first session to determine critical chokepoints in the system and their origins in infrastructure, operations, and policy.

12:30 Lunch and Keynote: The Canada-U.S. Border: Infrastructure, Commerce, and Values
The Honourable Alain Dudoit, Consul General of Canada

2:00 Breakout Session 3: Options for Relieving Capacity Constraints
The third session will integrate the discussions of the first two sessions; critical constraints will be considered in terms of their economic effects so that they may be relieved most efficiently. Both public- and private-sector action will be considered.

3:15 Break

3:30 Summary of Observations and Next Steps
To close the day's events, all participants will reconvene. The facilitators will present the results of the discussions to the entire group. Collectively, the participants will select critical issues and identify the next steps to relieving capacity constraints in the Canadian and U.S. freight transport systems.

APPENDIX B

Comments of Ambassador Alain Dudoit, Canadian Consul General, Los Angeles

Introduction

This conference is very timely. It is addressing a subject that is at the forefront of policy discussions over transportation, globalization, and the North American economy, in both Canada and the United States.

In these opening remarks, I would like to offer a series of observations, from the Canadian government's vantage point, on the challenges we are facing—in Canada, in the United States, in North America—to our transportation infrastructure as a result of growing North American and transpacific trade.

Transpacific trade is growing rapidly, spurred by the emergence of powerful economic actors such as China and Asia. Growing trade with China and other Asian economies means new business opportunities, but also poses growing strains on our transport networks.

Both in Canada and the United States, we are feeling that impact strongly. Congestion and delays create economic and environmental costs. There is real concern in the transportation world that our current infrastructure—ports, rail, roads—is inadequate to handle the projected increase in freight traffic.

Within North America itself, let's also not forget the huge role that NAFTA [the North American Free Trade Agreement] has played in stimulating trade and investment flows. This, too, has and still is placing strains on our transportation infrastructure and in reshaping our continental economy.

We also all know that infrastructure development takes time. Ports and highways cannot be built overnight—far from it—and, in many cases, there is simply no room for further expansion of such facilities, due to their being in highly populated areas or because of geography.

So, while we need to plan for long-term infrastructure requirements, we need to take steps in the short and medium terms to address and resolve transport bottlenecks, improve regulatory cooperation, make better use of information technology, develop better intermodal facilities, and make sure our borders truly are both secure and efficient.

We will also need to adopt a slightly different world view. Just as our governments and the private sector have adapted to the twin challenges of security and efficiency post-9/11, now we also need to make a similar paradigm shift to accommodate the economic challenges (and opportunities) posed by the emergence of China and India, principally. In this new paradigm, transportation policies will have to meet the demands of globalization and global supply chains, as well as security and efficiency, not to mention the equally important goals of environmental sustainability, public-private partnerships, and community involvement. To put it mildly, it is an ambitious agenda.

Canada-U.S. Overview

A few words are in order about the overall Canada-U.S. relationship. This relationship has greatly contributed to the prosperity of both countries. We share the world's largest and most comprehensive bilateral trading relationship, with more than $1.8 billion in trade crossing the Canada-U.S. border each day. In 2004, Canada's trade with the United States totalled $680 billion, surpassing Canada's trade with all other countries combined. Canada's trade with the United States is responsible for 52 percent of our gross domestic product. The United States represents roughly four-fifths of Canada's exports and two-thirds of our imports. Canada, in return, is a larger market for U.S. goods than all 25 countries of the European Union, which has over 15 times the Canadian population, combined.

For Canada, a strong transportation relationship is a key component of Canada-U.S. economic relations and, therefore, of Canadian prosperity.

This relationship is as complex as it is important. Much of our trade is the result of intricate supply chains managed by transnational corporations whose plants and suppliers are distributed throughout North America (including Mexico) and around the world. These firms, in particular the automotive industry, often work on the basis of just-in-time production, whereby suppliers must be prepared to meet, in a timely manner, assembly plants' needs for inputs used in their production processes. Just-in-time production requires seamless, reliable and integrated transportation systems, as well as an efficient border.

Moreover, just as our two economies are increasingly integrated across many sectors, so too are our transportation systems and infrastructure.

Approximately 36,000 trucks cross the border between Canada and the United States each day. In terms of value, trucks carried 62 percent of total trade between Canada and the United States in 2004, followed by rail (18 percent), pipeline (11 percent), air (6 percent), and marine (3 percent). In 2004, over 13 million trucks and almost 60 million cars crossed the land border (two-way traffic). Nearly 80 percent of Canada-U.S. trade (value) carried by trucks was concentrated at six border crossing points: Windsor/Ambassador Bridge, Fort Erie/Niagara Falls, Sarnia, and Lansdowne in Ontario; Lacolle in Quebec; and the Pacific Highway in British Columbia.

Such intensity in the flow of traffic has been made possible by the high degree of integration between the Canadian and U.S. transportation systems. Highways and rail lines cross borders and link with vast networks in both countries. In the marine mode, much traffic comes through Canadian ports destined for the United States and vice versa. Air passengers travel to international destinations from Canada and the United States using both countries as gateways, with Canadian passengers travelling to the United States having been precleared by U.S. customs in the largest Canadian airports.

This interdependence is manifest in the numerous cross-border, north-south trade and transportation corridors that exist, seeking to improve infrastructure, coordination among governments, and commercial exchanges among businesses. Some examples include the "International Mobility and Trade Corridor" in the Cascade Gateway, the "North America Super Corridor Coalition" in the centre of the continent, and the "Atlantica" economic region linking Atlantic Canada and the northeast United States.

We are working with the United States in marine commerce as well. For example, jointly, we are studying the future of the Great Lakes–St. Lawrence Seaway system, looking at its marine traffic and trade growth potential. It is a vital marine gateway or corridor for Canada and the United States that is not being used to its full potential.

Short-sea shipping is another area of focus, and one with potential benefits to alleviate at least some of the road-borne freight that concerns us. To this end, Canada and the United States jointly are hosting a Short Seas Shipping Conference in Vancouver, April 18–20. That conference will examine the potential role of short-sea shipping in the wider context of the integrated North American transportation system.

Borders

The efficiency of movement at border crossings is crucial to the Canadian economy's competitiveness. An important element of the Canada-U.S. bilateral transportation relationship is the heightened focus, since September 11, 2001, on security, which has resulted in increased border management challenges and contributed to congestion.

In the aftermath of September 11, 2001, the Canadian and U.S. governments partnered to enhance border security and to facilitate the flow of goods and people. Some major developments include the signing of the Smart Border Action Plan in late 2001; the establishment of the Free and Secure Trade (FAST) program, which offers expedited clearance processes for eligible goods to preauthorized importers, carriers, and drivers; and the NEXUS Programs, which simplify border crossings for preapproved, low-risk travellers.

In this context, I would like to underline the importance that Canada places on the Security and Prosperity Partnership (SPP), which is a trilateral agreement between Canada, the United States, and Mexico that explores opportunities to move beyond NAFTA and the Canada-U.S. Smart Border process to a comprehensive trilateral North American agenda. The SPP is chock full of good initiatives, bilateral and trilateral, aimed at improving North American economic cooperation and competitiveness through smarter regulations, harmonized standards, and liberalized rules.

Pacific Gateway Strategy

Of particular interest to you in California will be the "Pacific Gateway Strategy," one of the most exciting initiatives in the transportation and trade nexus in Canada in a long time.

It was announced last fall by the former Government of Prime Minister Paul Martin. In short, the rise of emerging markets such as China and India makes it a national priority to maximize the effectiveness of the Pacific Gateway and ensure that the Canadian economy is taking maximum advantage of it. That requires a new, integrated approach to a wide range of interconnected issues, including, but going well beyond, transportation infrastructure.

Canada's Pacific Gateway is a multimodal network of transportation infrastructure focused on trade with Asia. It is comprised of interconnected public and privately owned assets, including ports, airports, and rail and road systems.

Changing trade patterns associated with emerging markets are predicted to result in significant growth in traffic through Canada's Pacific Gateway. By 2020, container cargo coming through British Columbian ports is projected to increase by up to 300 percent, from 1.8 million containers to between 5 and 7 million containers. The value of this trade is projected to reach $75 billion by 2020, up from the current $35 billion. This increase would contribute $10.5 billion annually to the Canadian economy, including $3.5 billion beyond British Columbia. The trade increases are also projected to result in 178-percent growth in direct jobs by 2020, from 18,000 to 50,000.

The rapid rise of China as a trading power directs particular attention to both the challenges and opportunities associated with Canada's Pacific orientation. Canada is uniquely positioned to take advantage of emerging opportunities in China and other Asia-Pacific countries including India and Korea. The Pacific Gateway also benefits considerably from a population that enjoys strong cultural connections with the Asia-Pacific through heritage, family ties, businesses, and investments.

The proximity of Canada's West Coast ports to Asian markets offers a sailing time advantage of roughly two days over all others in the western hemisphere. Canadian railways offer among the most affordable freight rates in North America and the country's trucking sector is also highly competitive and efficient, both in Canada and in transborder markets. As a result, a significant portion of the goods handled in Canada's West Coast ports are coming from, or destined for, the United States. In 2003, the Port of Vancouver and Fraser Port handled close to 250,000 containers that were destined to or coming from the United States, and this is predicted to grow to almost 1 million containers by 2020.

In addition, significant containerized traffic passing through the new container terminal being developed by the Port of Prince Rupert will likely be destined to or originating from the U.S. Midwest. Clearly, a strong foundation exists on which to further develop Canada's Pacific Gateway as the crossroads between North America and Asia.

The opportunities are great, but so are the challenges. Recent trade flow increases have strained existing transportation infrastructure capacity on the West Coast. Specifically, the Port of Vancouver has experienced two periods of significant backlogs partly as a result of bottlenecks on the road network causing slowdowns in the British Columbia Lower Mainland and points further east. The rail network is also being challenged to meet rising demands. The port backlogs have resulted in freight diversion to other ports and are causing some shippers concern about the future reliability of West Coast ports, road and rail services, and infrastructure.

In addition to infrastructure capacity, gateway performance is also affected directly by a range of factors such as labour market issues, including skill shortages in critical fields such as longhaul trucking, operating practices in the supply chain, increasing pressures in border management, the regulatory and economic policies of all levels of government, and municipal land use policies and practices.

New Canadian Government

Before turning to a few concluding remarks, I wanted to say a few words about our new government, led by Prime Minister Stephen Harper, elected in the general election of January 23.

Clearly, an important priority of any Canadian government is to maintain and improve relations with the United States. Mr. Harper's government will seek to do just that, and I fully expect the government in the coming weeks to focus on how we can do even better at cross-border management and security cooperation.

Two early signs from the cabinet appointed by Prime Minister Harper show that the new government understands the critical importance of transportation to the economy.

The first sign was that the new Minister of Transport, Lawrence Cannon, will also have responsibility for infrastructure, which is intended to "better link urban, interprovincial and international infrastructure development." This is a clear reference to the need to ensure that, in Canada, we have sufficient highways and ports to link to our major trading partners, including, obviously, the United States.

The second sign was that the new Minister of International Trade, David Emerson, will also have responsibility for the Pacific Gateway. This is a good indication that the new government recognizes the importance of improving Canada's Pacific Gateway and is prepared to work with the many stakeholders involved to do just that.

Concluding Remarks

In my comments, I have tried to identify some of the larger, macro challenges and opportunities we see facing freight transportation in North America in the coming years: secure and efficient borders, security, trade gateways, corridors.

Clearly, Canada needs good transportation linkages to the U.S. economy, as well as secure access for our goods and services. These are fundamental to our economic well-being.

But, as I noted earlier, our economies and transportation networks are increasingly interdependent and integrated. NAFTA has contributed to this; growing trade with Asia will further the integration. Our economies therefore face similar challenges and opportunities, and we will need to work together.

There are many ways to do this: close collaboration in the development of border infrastructure; making our borders both more secure and more efficient; smart transportation systems; using alternative forms of transport, such as short-sea shipping; and better intermodal connections.

APPENDIX C

Attendees of Workshop on Increasing the Capacity of Freight Transportation

Workshop Participants

Jane Beseda, Group Vice President and General Manager, Toyota Customer Services Division (then Vice President, North American Parts and Accessories), Toyota Motor Sales USA, Inc.

Larry Breisinger, Vice President, Supply Chain Logistics, H. J. Heinz Co., North America

Jeff Brown, Consultant, Senate Office of Research

The Honourable Alain Dudoit, Consul General of Canada, Los Angeles

William Ferguson, Group Security Officer and Security Director, NYK Line North America Inc.

Gerald Fisher, Partner, Lord Bissell and Brook LLP

Carol Hoffman, Chief, Strategic Initiatives Division, U.S. Transportation Command

Pam Johnson, Cultural and Academic Relations Officer, Canadian Consulate General, Los Angeles

Ken Lewenza, President, CAW Local 444, Canadian Auto Workers Union

Kirk Lindsey, President, Brite Transportation Systems

Ted Mackay, Counsellor, Transportation, Canadian Embassy, Washington, D.C.

James McCarthy, Chief, Regional Planning and Public Transportation, California Department of Transportation

Tony Minyon, National Logistics Manager, Toyota Motor Sales USA, Inc.

Randal Mullett, Vice President, Government Relations, CNF Inc.

William Murnighan, National Staff Representative, Canadian Auto Workers Union

Richard Nordahl, Chief, Office of Goods Movement, California Department of Transportation

Eric Pelletier, Consul, Political, Economic, Public Affairs, Canadian Consulate, Los Angeles

Eugene Pentimonti, Senior Vice President, Government Relations, Maersk, Inc.

Larry Rogers, Managing Director, Strategic Planning and Customer Quality, FedEx Freight

William Rooney, Managing Director, American Headquarters, Hanjin Shipping

Sandra Scott, Director, International Relations, YRC Worldwide

Amgad Shehata, Vice President, UPS Canada

Seth Stodder, Senior Counsel, Akin Gump Strauss Hauer and Feld, LLP

Rod Van Bebber, Senior Vice President, Distribution, Unified Western Grocers, Inc.

Marianne Venieris, Executive Director, Center for International Trade and Transportation, California State University, Long Beach

Janet Weiss, General Manager, Grain, Canadian Pacific Railway

Captain Paul Wiedenhoeft, Deputy Commander, Alternate Captain of the Port, and Alternate Federal Maritime Security Coordinator, U.S. Coast Guard Los Angeles–Long Beach

Michael Zachary, Director, Port of Tacoma

RAND Participants

Rae Archibald, Interim Dean, Pardee RAND Graduate School

Myles Collins, Fellow, Pardee RAND Graduate School

Mark Dawson, Director of Development, International Programs, RAND

Fred Kipperman, Deputy Director of Development, RAND

Naveen Mandava, Fellow, Pardee RAND Graduate School

Nancy Young Moore, Senior Management Scientist, RAND

Christopher Ordowich, Fellow, Pardee RAND Graduate School

David Ortiz, Engineer, RAND

Michael Rich, Executive Vice President, RAND

K. Jack Riley, Deputy Director, RAND Infrastructure, Safety, and Environment

Bianca Roberts, Director of Development, Pardee RAND Graduate School

Paul Sorensen, Associate Operations Researcher, RAND

Elizabeth Stacey, Executive Director of Development, RAND

Martin Wachs, Director, RAND Transportation, Space, and Technology

Brian Weatherford, Fellow, Pardee RAND Graduate School

Henry Willis, Policy Researcher, RAND

APPENDIX D

Annotated Bibliography of Recent Studies and Plans for Addressing Issues of Freight Transport Capacity

California Marine and Intermodal Transportation System Advisory Council (CALMITSAC), *Growth of California Ports: Opportunities and Challenges: An Interim Report to the California State Legislature*, January 2006. As of March 29, 2006:
http://www.cunninghamreport.com/3136CALMITSAC.pdf
Growth of California Ports: Opportunities and Challenges is a report to the California state legislature that summarizes expert opinion on strategies for improving the efficiency, reliability, velocity, capacity, and security of the marine transport system in the state of California. The report makes 39 recommendations to the legislature, in seven broad categories, all of which are aimed at addressing the various constraints on the growth of California's ports that stem from institutional, statutory, community, and environmental factors. The report includes a list of proposed infrastructure projects at each port, along with costs, as well as a list of potential operational improvements.

California Marine and Intermodal Transportation System Advisory Council, Northern California Marine Transportation System Advisory Council, and Southern California Marine Transportation System Advisory Council, "California Marine Transportation System Infrastructure Needs," March 11, 2003. As of March 29, 2006:
http://www.mtsnac.org/docs/CALMITSAC_%20MTS_%20Infrastructure_Needs%2010_22_03.htm
The "California Marine Transportation System Infrastructure Needs" report, written by three CALMITSAC organizations, focuses on the ports and supporting inland transport systems in California. It was intended to build on the Global Gateways Development Program and was timed to help inform Congress during the Transportation Equity Act reauthorization process. This report makes four policy recommendations: Recognize the national importance of California's ports, support the California marine transport system and the supporting multimodal infrastructure with federal funding sources, help to mitigate the local environmental effects, and affirm that improving access to ports is a matter of national security. The report also presents a list of 25 high-priority infrastructure projects in need of immediate funding, along with two appendixes that address the comprehensive infrastructure needs of the California marine transport system.

Office of the Governor of the State of California, "Governor's Strategic Growth Plan Protects Stable Funding for Transportation Improvement Projects," undated Web page. As of March 29, 2006:
http://www.strategicgrowthplan.com/transportation/
The Strategic Growth Plan is the first phase of a 20-year infrastructure plan for the state of California proposed by Governor Arnold Schwarzenegger. A significant portion of the $222 billion financing plan is devoted to transportation, but only a fraction of that is for improving freight transportation. The plan proposes to spend $15 billion directly on trade infrastructure and an additional $2 billion on environmental mitigation at ports; of that $17 billion, $4 billion will come from general obligation bond issues. Presumably, some of the $53 billion in highway investments and $3 billion in spending on intelligent transportation technology will also generate benefits to the freight transport system. No individual projects have been identified; specific projects will likely be finalized during negotiations over the budget bill and the bills authorizing the bond issues.

Martin E. Robins and Anne Strauss-Wieder, "Principles for a U.S. Public Freight Agenda in a Global Economy," Washington, D.C.: The Brookings Institution, January 2006. As of March 29, 2006:
http://www.brookings.edu/metro/pubs/20060117_freightsystems.htm

Robins and Strauss-Wieder recommend "guiding principles" for developing public policy on freight transportation: Use a systems approach to develop and fund federal and state freight transport policy, and promote increased coordination and collaboration among public agencies and the private sector in freight transportation. The authors conclude with five policy recommendations based on these guiding principles. This paper is a concise discussion of the national freight transport challenge and the fundamental issues voiced at the Volcker workshop.

Security and Prosperity Partnership of North America, undated homepage. As of March 29, 2006:
http://www.spp.gov/
SPP is a trilateral agreement among Canada, Mexico, and the United States that provides the framework needed to increase security and enhance prosperity through greater cooperation and information sharing. A report to leaders, written by officials from the three governments, outlines the large number of collaborative initiatives addressing common prosperity and security that had been completed at the time. That report also outlines "key themes and initiatives" to seek—for example, regulation streamlining, continental free trade, collaboration to enhance industrial competitiveness on the continent, faster and more efficient border crossings, environmental improvement, and enhancement of border security.

Southern California Association of Governments, *Southern California Regional Strategy for Goods Movement: A Plan for Action*, Los Angeles, Calif.: SCAG, March 2005. As of March 29, 2006:
http://www.scag.ca.gov/goodsmove/pdf/GoodsmovePaper0305.pdf
Southern California Regional Strategy for Goods Movement: A Plan for Action states five principles for guiding efforts to improve the freight transport system in the Southern California region, an area of significance for national and continental goods movement. In this plan, the Southern California Association of Governments (SCAG) calls for state and federal assistance to help the region mitigate the externalities associated with goods movement and to help fund freight transport system improvements so that funding for other, local transport system investments is not affected. The plan outlines a comprehensive, multimodal strategy to ease current constraints and meet future demand. This includes an initial list of 18 improvements, an estimate of how much money is needed to build them, and seven potential funding solutions. In addition, the plan discusses goods movement initiatives that SCAG is currently implementing.

State of California, "Global Gateways Development Program," January 2002. As of March 29, 2006:
http://www.dot.ca.gov/hq/tpp/offices/ogm/globalgateways.htm
The Global Gateways Development Program report identifies high-priority seaport, airport, and border access and intrastate transportation system improvements for California state, federal, and other funding. To this end, the plan identifies four major international trade regions in California and all of the transportation facilities that carry international freight. A table presents deficiencies in the freight transport system and recommends infrastructure projects to improve the system. The report also outlines the challenges in moving goods in California today; the administration's overall goods movement goals, policies, and desired performance outcomes; and funding options for goods movement improvements.

U.S. Department of Transportation, Under Secretary of Transportation for Policy, *Framework for a National Freight Policy*, Washington, D.C.: DOT, April 10, 2006. As of March 29, 2006:
http://ostpxweb.dot.gov/freight_policy_framework.html
Framework for a National Freight Policy outlines seven objectives for improving the U.S. freight transport system: Improve operations, add physical capacity, use pricing, reduce or remove statutory or regulatory barriers, identify and address emerging needs, maximize safety and security, and better manage environmental and community impacts. For each objective, the framework details strategies and tactics that might be used to achieve those objectives. This plan is not intended to establish federal policy, but to initiate communication and collaboration with the private sector and other public organizations.

Waterfront Coalition, *National Marine Container Transportation System: A Call to Action*, Washington, D.C., May 2005. As of March 29, 2006:
http://www.portmod.org/INDUSTRY%20INFO/NATIONAL%20MARINE%20CONTAINER%20TRANSPORTATION%20SYSTEM.pdf
National Marine Container Transportation System: A Call to Action is a policy document prepared by the Waterfront Coalition, an advocacy organization calling for increased port and freight transport system capacity in the United States. The document is organized according to six broad recommendations: Improve

the productivity and efficiency of American ports, encourage the development of alternative Pacific ports, invest in intermodal rail, increase investment in freight transport and do so with input from the shipping industry, improve trade and transportation forecasting, and promote and improve port infrastructure on the East Coast and Gulf Coast. The document identifies specific action items and infrastructure projects related to each of the recommendations to form a framework for the development of a national freight transport policy.

References

American Society of Civil Engineers, *2005 Report Card on America's Infrastructure*, Reston, Va.: American Society of Civil Engineers, 2005.

Audi, Tamara, "Inspectors: Security Lags When Traffic Jams," *Detroit Free Press*, March 29, 2006.

Breen, Bill, "Living in Dell Time," *Fast Company*, November 2004, p. 86.

Byrd, Erlinda, "Rules for Improving Cargo Security," *Customs and Border Protection Today*, March 2004. As of December 7, 2006:
http://www.cbp.gov/xp/CustomsToday/2004/March/Other/rules_cargosecurity.xml

California Environmental Protection Agency, *Goods Movement Action Plan: Phase I, Foundations*, Sacramento, Calif.: California Environmental Protection Agency, California Business, Transportation and Housing Agency, 2005. As of December 7, 2006:
http://www.arb.ca.gov/gmp/docs/finalgmpplan090205.pdf

California Environmental Protection Agency Air Resources Board, *Draft Emission Reduction Plan for Ports and International Goods Movement in California*, Sacramento, Calif.: California Environmental Protection Agency, Air Resources Board, 2005.

California Marine and Intermodal Transportation System Advisory Council, *Growth of California Ports: Opportunities and Challenges: An Interim Report to the California State Legislature*, January 2006. As of March 29, 2006:
http://www.cunninghamreport.com/3136CALMITSAC.pdf

California Marine and Intermodal Transportation System Advisory Council, Northern California Marine Transportation System Advisory Council, and Southern California Marine Transportation System Advisory Council, "California Marine Transportation System Infrastructure Needs," March 11, 2003. As of March 29, 2006:
http://www.mtsnac.org/docs/CALMITSAC_%20MTS_%20Infrastructure_Needs%2010_22_03.htm

City of Louisville, "Louisville's UPS Hub to Nearly Double in Capacity," press release, May 17, 2006. As of December 7, 2006:
http://www.louisvilleky.gov/Mayor/News/2006/51706upsexpansion.htm

Finnegan, William, "Watching the Waterfront: Mobsters, Terrorists, and the Docks of New York Harbor," *The New Yorker*, June 19, 2006, p. 54.

Foschi, Alga D., "The Coast Port Industry in the U.S.A.: A Key Factor in the Process of Economic Growth," Department of Economics discussion paper no. 46, Pisa, Italy: Dipartimento di Scienze Economiche, Universita di Pisa, December 2004. As of December 7, 2006:
http://papers.ssrn.com/sol3/papers.cfm?abstract_id=720265

Frittelli, John, *Hurricane Katrina: Shipping Disruptions*, Washington, D.C.: Congressional Research Service, Library of Congress, RS22257, 2005. As of December 7, 2006:
http://library.nps.navy.mil/uhtbin/hyperion/CRS-RS22257.pdf

Goldstein, Amy, "Strapped States Try New Route, Lease Toll Roads to Foreign Firms," *The Washington Post*, June 14, 2006, p. A01.

Hall, Peter V., "'We'd Have to Sink the Ships': Impact Studies and the 2002 West Coast Port Lockout," *Economic Development Quarterly*, Vol. 18, No. 4, November 2004, pp. 354–367.

International Maritime Organization, "FAQ on ISPS Code and Maritime Security," undated Web page. As of December 7, 2006:
http://www.imo.org
via Newsroom | Maritime Security

Knatz, Geraldine, "Has the Time Come to Consider National Port Planning?" paper presented at Transportation Research Board 2005 Summer Conference, Boston, Mass., July 10–12, 2005. As of December 7, 2006:
http://onlinepubs.trb.org/webmedia/trbweb/midknatz/index.htm

Koraleski, Jack, "Are We in a 'Perfect Storm'?" paper presented at Council of Supply Chain Management Professionals 2005 Annual Conference, San Diego, Calif., October 24–26, 2005.

Lofgren, Christopher B., "A Perfect Storm in Transportation," paper presented at Council of Supply Chain Management Professionals 2005 Annual Conference, San Diego, Calif., October 24–26, 2005.

Machalaba, Daniel, "Making Tracks: Big Railroads Race to Cross U.S. Again," *The Wall Street Journal*, December 28, 2004, p. A1.

Martonosi, Susan E., David S. Ortiz, and Henry H. Willis, "Evaluating the Viability of 100 Per Cent Container Inspection at America's Ports," in Harry Ward Richardson, Peter Gordon, and James Elliott Moore, eds., *The Economic Impacts of Terrorist Attacks*, Cheltenham, UK, and Northampton, Mass.: Edward Elgar, 2005, pp. 218–241.

Mecham, Michael, "A Bit Heavy; At This Stage, Boeing Says It's Not Worried About 787 Weight," *Aviation Week and Space Technology*, April 3, 2006, p. 26.

Mongelluzzo, Bill, "LA–Long Beach Volume Overwhelms Inland Traffic," *The Journal of Commerce*, December 6, 2004.

National Research Council, *Surviving Supply Chain Integration: Strategies for Small Manufacturers*, Washington, D.C.: National Academy Press, 2000.

Njord, John R., and Michael D. Meyer, *Critical Issues in Transportation*, Washington, D.C.: Transportation Research Board of the National Academies, January 20, 2006. As of December 7, 2006:
http://onlinepubs.trb.org/onlinepubs/general/CriticalIssues06.pdf

Office of the Governor of the State of California, "Governor's Strategic Growth Plan Protects Stable Funding for Transportation Improvement Projects," undated Web page. As of March 29, 2006:
http://www.strategicgrowthplan.com/transportation/

PierPASS, undated homepage. As of December 7, 2006:
http://www.pierpass.org/

Pinkston, Elizabeth, *Freight Rail Transportation: Long-Term Issues*, Washington, D.C.: Congress of the United States, Congressional Budget Office, 2006. As of December 7, 2006:
http://www.cbo.gov/ftpdocs/70xx/doc7021/01-17-Rail.pdf

Port of Long Beach, *Green Port Program: Quarterly Report #3*, Long Beach, Calif.: The Port of Long Beach, December 13, 2005. As of December 7, 2006:
http://www.polb.com/civica/filebank/blobdload.asp?BlobID=2559

"The Right Kind of Security: It's a Bad Idea to Inspect Each of the 11 Million Containers That Enter This Country Every Year," editorial, *The Washington Post*, June 1, 2006, p. A18.

Robins, Martin E., and Anne Strauss-Wieder, "Principles for a U.S. Public Freight Agenda in a Global Economy," Washington, D.C.: The Brookings Institution, January 2006. As of March 29, 2006: http://www.brookings.edu/metro/pubs/20060117_freightsystems.pdf

Ryan, Sid, "Most Important Link; The 76-Year-Old Ambassador Bridge Handles One Quarter of Canada/U.S. Trade Annually," *The Toronto Sun*, October 7, 2005. As of June 5, 2006: http://torontosun.canoe.ca/News/Columnists/Ryan_Sid/2005/10/07/1251730.html

Schoch, Deborah, "The State: Port Panel Chief Has Plenty to Unload," *Los Angeles Times*, January 15, 2006, p. A1.

Schwartz, Sam, *Windsor Gateway: What Now?* New York: Sam Schwartz Engineering PLLC, 2005.

Security and Prosperity Partnership of North America, undated homepage. As of December 7, 2006: http://www.spp.gov

Seidl, Jason H., and Jagdeep S. Ghuman, *Shippers Speak Out: Rails Dinged on Pricing and Service*, New York: Credit Suisse, 2006.

Southern California Association of Governments, *Southern California Regional Strategy for Goods Movement: A Plan for Action*, Los Angeles, Calif.: SCAG, March 2005. As of March 29, 2006: http://www.scag.ca.gov/goodsmove/pdf/GoodsmovePaper0305.pdf

State of California, "Global Gateways Development Program," January 2002. As of March 29, 2006: http://www.dot.ca.gov/hq/tpp/offices/ogm/globalgateways.htm

Tran, Hien, *Appendix A: Quantification of the Health Impacts and Economic Valuation of Air Pollution from Ports and Goods Movement in California*, Sacramento, Calif.: California Air Resources Board, March 21, 2006. As of December 7, 2006:
http://www.arb.ca.gov/planning/gmerp/march21plan/appendix_a.pdf

Transportation Security Administration, "Transportation Worker Identification Credential Program: Frequently Asked Questions," undated Web page. As of December 7, 2006: http://www.tsa.gov/what_we_do/layers/twic/twic_faqs.shtm

U.S. Coast Guard, "MTSA-ISPS Information Site," undated Web page. As of December 7, 2006: http://www.uscg.mil/HQ/G-M/MP/mtsa.shtml

U.S. Customs and Border Protection, "Customs-Trade Partnership Against Terrorism (C-TPAT): Partnership to Secure the Supply Chain," undated Web page (a). As of December 7, 2006: http://www.cbp.gov/xp/cgov/import/commercial_enforcement/ctpat/

———, "Keeping Cargo Safe: Container Security Initiative," undated Web page (b). As of December 7, 2006:
http://www.cbp.gov/xp/cgov/border_security/international_activities/csi/

U.S. Department of Homeland Security, *Secure Seas, Open Ports: Keeping Our Waters Safe, Secure and Open for Business*, Washington, D.C.: DHS, June 21, 2004. As of December 7, 2006: http://www.dhs.gov/xlibrary/assets/DHSPortSecurityFactSheet-062104.pdf

U.S. Department of Transportation, Under Secretary of Transportation for Policy, *Framework for a National Freight Policy*, Washington, D.C.: DOT, April 10, 2006a. As of June 21, 2006: http://ostpxweb.dot.gov/freight_policy_framework.html

———, "Secretary of Transportation Norman Y. Mineta Convenes First Meeting of National Commission on Surface Transportation Funding Saying It Has Opportunity to Make a 'Historic Transition,'" press release, May 24, 2006b. As of December 7, 2006:
http://www.dot.gov/affairs/dot6506.htm

U.S. House of Representatives, Committee on Homeland Security, Subcommittee on Economic Security, Infrastructure Protection, and Cybersecurity, *Fact Sheet: H.R. 4954: The SAFE Port Act*, undated. As of

December 7, 2006:
http://homeland.house.gov/news/latestNews/20060314-PortSecurityLegislation/TP-SAFEPortAct032906.pdf

Waterfront Coalition, *National Marine Container Transportation System: A Call to Action*, Washington, D.C., May 2005. As of March 29, 2006:
http://www.portmod.org/INDUSTRY%20INFO/NATIONAL%20MARINE%20CONTAINER%20TRANSPORTATION%20SYSTEM.pdf

White, Ronald D., "Global Capital: Shipping Industry Sees Signs of Slowing," *Los Angeles Times*, June 10, 2006, p. C1.

Widdows, Ron, *Briefing on Port and Intermodal Transport Issues*, Washington, D.C.: U.S. Department of Transportation, 2005.

Womack, James P., and Daniel T. Jones, *Lean Thinking: Banish Waste and Create Wealth in Your Corporation*, New York: Simon and Schuster, 1996.